Aquakineticist

Aquakineticist

Poems

Abby N. Lewis

RESOURCE *Publications* • Eugene, Oregon

AQUAKINETICIST
Poems

Resource Publications
An Imprint of Wipf and Stock Publishers
199 W. 8th Ave., Suite 3
Eugene, OR 97401

www.wipfandstock.com

PAPERBACK ISBN: 979-8-3852-3108-9
HARDCOVER ISBN: 979-8-3852-3109-6
EBOOK ISBN: 979-8-3852-3110-2

VERSION NUMBER 021725

This collection is dedicated to my own mental health journey

Clouds, after all, are more
than bearers of rain. The infinite sea
moves inside us

—Rita Dove,
Sonata Mulattica

Contents

III.

IV.

V.

Acknowledgments

The following poems were previously published, sometimes in slightly different forms, in the publications listed below:

Across the Margin: "Small Hands, Bad Back" and "crimson thoughts"

The Allegheny Review: "Viola da Gamba" and "The Bridge"

Cheat River Review: "Pinecone"

The Crambo: "Prisoner" and "Palm Up, Fingers Curled"

The Mildred Haun Review: "Song of Habit" and "Tsunami"

The Mockingbird: "4th of July," "0.6 inches," "In-Between," "Mirror Perceptions," and "Sentries of the Cemetery"

Outrageous Fortune: "The Essence of Lounging"

Red Eft Review: "Smoke Break Outside Swann's Chapel Church," "Picture it," and "Rainelle, West Virginia"

Red Mud Review: "Snakes and Stones"

Sanctuary: "Snippets—I Can't" and "The Big Texan Steak Ranch"

Sigma Tau Delta Rectangle: "Trout Fishing" and "The Flood"

The Tennessee Magazine: "Our Late Grandmother's House"

Some poems in this collection also previously appeared in small chapbooks from the following small presses:

This Fluid Journey, Finishing Line Press, September 2018

Palm Up, Fingers Curled, Plan B Press, May 2023

I.

In the Beginning

Talking and driving down
                Sevierville back roads
      late at night,

we did not see the wayward
      limb, heavily adorned with leaves,
                until it was almost upon us.

You swerved,
      rescuing us last-minute,
  and we sat in stunned
          silence—

til we looked at each other and laughed.

We were young and fearless;
      we had more time ahead of us
          than leaves on that branch—
              and we were burning stars.

We laughed
      and laughed
and swerved
      past obstacles—

racehorses in the Milky Way,
      fluid and untraceable.

Days of the Dinosaurs

When the summertime grass grew high,
my sister and I would grab our plastic dinosaurs,
venture out, and let our toys explore uncharted lands.
Mother stood at the window, watched our hair
dance with rays of light as we chortled together;
our voices filled the natural pauses,
creating a new sound in the breaths between.
Together, we bested Time.
No matter how long we lingered,
night never arrived,
and the sun never tired of lightening our hair.

Smoke Break Outside Swann's Chapel Church

He sits in his Lincoln, smokes a cigarette
and thinks of his wife.
No doubt she has a list of chores for him
as long as his hours spent at work:
the wall in the bedroom needs a facelift,
the pool could use sanitizing
after the grandkid's last visit, the second
guest room door squeaks.
No one ever stays in that room anyway.
Then she'll complain
she forgot the butter for the brownies,
could he buy some?
He rehearses how to tell her no,
sticks a hand out the door
and taps the rolled paper. Eventually,
he smothers the butt
on the dash—the Lincoln coughs to life,
and as he pulls away,
exhaust smoke rises in the rearview mirror
to blend with the alabaster wall.

Gateway Gratification

I smoked Kings candy cigarettes as a child,
holding the chalk-like stick between two
      fingers, an imitation of success.

I ate bright powder off a white stick and drank
sparkling juice from a wine bottle, learning
      to crave the feeling of glass against my lips.

As a young adult, I bought bright placebo
drugs in a clear container, relishing
      their chatter in my mouth.

I chewed pseudo tobacco made from livestock,
a permanent circular crease in the pocket of my
      jeans, the illusion of greatness.

I was given the tools of destruction
before I could even spell the word.
      Now I have to learn bigger words.

Small Hands, Bad Back

Dad's back is inflamed;
I laugh as he shuffles into the living room,
bowed as a caveman tending his fire.
But the laughter is only to yank the fear back.

I separated from my parents at the store once
to use the bathroom. When I returned,
Mom said, *She found us already.* I replied,
It was easy to find the giant man.

Back then, he stood tall, towering over everything, fatherly sky-
scraper.

Now, each episode beats my father nearer
to the ground. The chiropractor visits
no longer work like they used to.
There is no magic touch left in those fingers.

The grocery store becomes more labyrinthine
each visit. In the canned foods isle,
Popeye and the Green Giant conspire
over the squeak of damaged wheels
like skipping records, flexing
their bulging muscles. I knock Popeye
into the cart, taking care he lands on his
face, flaunt my own untatted muscles back
at the green man left on the shelf,
a promise for another day.

Ageing is never graceful—
I would cure my father if I could,
massage the spine until it's
powerful as any ancestral tree.
But there is no magic in
these small hands either.

Snakes and Stones

She was a wild child, my sister. At four,
she hopped on her red and yellow tricycle
and peddled halfway round the block, naked
as the day she arrived. Grandmother phoned,
demanded how Mother could let Chelsea ride bare,
on full display for the entire neighborhood. Mother
let the gust of Grandmother's words pass over her ear,
calm as ever. She didn't even go after my sister,
let her return the same way she left.

Mother knew the house was a crib Chelsea
would not be confined to; its intolerable
prison-bar view kept her from making friends—
until the day she found a garden snake
hidden in the rock garden out front.
It was no longer than the space
between her wrist and the tip of her pinky.
My sister understood a house of rocks
was not the same as a house of flowers,
so she kept it by her bed—in a shoe box
filled with grass, clovers, and dandelions—
until Mother had a dream the snake
offered her child a killing bite.

We let it go the next morning.
It took a week before my sister's eyes
dried completely. In the months after,
she was often found curled asleep against the belly
of our golden retriever, her fine honey-blonde hair
splayed over the dog's coat like an added shawl.

Waning

In the summertime, Mother would lie
on the back deck for hours,
        breed freckles on her arms.

When she finally returned to the shade,
I stared at the stranger
        who called herself my life giver.

Grandmother, too, had unusual freckles—
one in particular resembled
        the sliver of a moon. I imagined

I was the wolf, come to howl over how
she never seemed to give
        my words any merit.

I stared at the thumbnail-sized silent
judge on her forearm in every conversation,
        never receiving an answer.

Now, Mother's freckles bleed together
like wax from melted crayons, and
        I work to separate one

from the others, searching for that absent
sliver in my life, the moon
        that was never full enough.

For the Angel Lady

Every time you came to the grocery store,
you gave the cashier a wire angel secured
with a ribbon, always a different color.

I was lucky enough to get two little
blessings—brown and yellow. They
hang from the black window curtain

in my room, looped around the
employee name badge. I never
bothered to learn your name.

When you stopped walking through
the door, I could ask no one where
you had gone. Instead, I fingered the

wire memories that rested across from
my heart and marveled at how something
so coarse could feel so smooth.

Flashes

Thunder rocks the house, jolts me awake. From
the other room, I hear my sister jump out of bed.
In a moment, my door will open, and she will crawl
in beside me, wrap an arm around my waist, tell me
she is scared. I smile as another flash frames her
face in my doorway; I reach out a hand and pull her
under the covers with me, just like old times when
we shared a bunk bed. I was excited when Katie
moved out at eighteen because it meant I finally
got a room to myself, no more staring at the bowed
mattress above me. Chelsea used to wait until I was
settled before she would let one loose five feet from
my nostrils, then lean over the side rail and ask if I
could smell it yet. Other nights, we talked of things
we never mentioned during the day; how Mom and
Dad were yelling at each other more than they usually
did, that Katie's room smelled like cigarettes, whether
it was okay to still be a virgin at sixteen, if people could
tell. I rest my arm over hers and bring up the bunk bed
days. Another boom drowns out her reply, but her warm
breath on my hair tells me all I need to know.

The Bridge

Wooden boards softened by rain,
nibbled by passing termites who take
what lies beneath their feet. Sunken eyes
and creaky joints that now sigh underfoot.

Moss gazes at the underbelly of the bridge
as a shadow covers the light which seeps
between closed blinds. The water's whisper
grows to a timid babble as birds
adjust their wings in preparation for flight.

The child attached to the shadow pauses,
takes in the circular swampland to the left
where half-submerged logs imitate the perfect
curves of an alligator's brow—
the dense forest on the slope to the right, each tree
tilted forward like a child frozen mid-windmilled run
down the incline, nearly toppling over,
yet somehow still grounded.

Before her lies the house on cement stilts
with a deck in the back built more for support
than any sort of architectural appeal. The aged
woman who lives in the abandoned castle
watches the girl make her way through grass
that brushes her shoulders, as giddy
as the time when she was a child.

The woman is armed with baked goods to summon
the small spirit of both the past and the future
across the bridge and over the dusty threshold of her palace.
Like a ghost to a séance, the girl answers the unspoken
call of the twin crystal eyes, drawn to the concrete
presence of forgotten times.

Behind the girl, foxtails peek through the
chapped lips of the bridge, their mourning dance
pulled from them with each insistent tug of the wind.

Certified

I asked Mother once if my name had any
special origin, hoping for a grand story
that had to do with a long-dead relative
or perhaps a brave fictional character.

All she said, with a shrug of apology,
was, *No, I just liked the sound of it.*
I guess that means I'll have to compose
my own story—begin with the *A*—a

fitting letter. Transition into the stutter
of the double *B*s. Next is the *Y* that always
comes too soon. What of all the letters
hidden in the crevices? Mother said she

named me what she did instead of Abigale
because she knew she and others would shorten
it, so why condemn me to a life of correcting
teachers and friends, demanding a name that

was not mine by right? Grandmother disagreed.
She claimed it was not proper, that Mother
was just being lazy. Now, when people become
familiar with my company, they switch to Abigale,

a backfired attempt at intimacy.
Gently, I inform them the condensed
version is in fact the only version, as
written on the birth certificate.

Waiting for the Dead

Her frail eyes scan the paper.
Another day, another list. A
shaky finger traces the words
on the page, praying that she
won't see a familiar name,
familiar face.
Her finger reaches the last
black dot, hovering over the
space above it before lowering
it delicately to rest upon the ink.

She bows her head, and the
newspaper mimics the action
as she releases all the air she'd
held captive as she read. No one
she knows today. She'll
check again tomorrow.

Angel Food Cake

Hands sticky from the moist cake,
as soft as air, well worth the trudge
across the bridge and up the hill to
Grandma's house—the required
head bobbing fee of listening to her
talk of relatives in Ohio I've never
met. I also get a bag of trash to lug
to our house. Grandma can't afford
to pay the real trash man, but she
still places four silver quarters in
my hand—opposed to child labor
even after all these years.

The eating slows as I think of her,
trapped in her own home. She never
learned to drive, left her family to
follow her daughter, whose man had
the big idea to become an entrepreneur
in the second oldest town in Tennessee.
The cake lies heavy in my stomach,
feeling so different than it had in my
hands only moments ago. The only
remnants are sticky fingers that cling
to useless silver coins.

In-Between

Too big to simply carry to bed.
Too small to wake.
That nasty in-between
of adolescence where
even your parents don't know
how to treat you anymore.
So they let you lie
half-awake in the
back seat of the car,
convinced you'll
instinctively rise and
follow them inside
in a few minutes.

When you don't,
they pretend not
to notice, call you
cute in your
absence, as if you
were still that
three-year-old toddler
tripping through their house—
not the stranger
asleep
in the back seat of the car.

Memories Ablaze

We stand side by side, silhouetted against
the night as the flames eat away at our
house. A cloud of smoke rises from the
dining room, forsaken distress call. With
every second that passes, another memory
disintegrates—a journal from my elementary
days, a stuffed Jack Russell Terrier my sister
got when she was three, a clock of Elvis whose
pelvis will no longer swing in tandem with the
times. She reaches out her hand for mine, but I
pull her to me and let the dampness seep into
the fabric of my cotton shirt as the wind weaves
ashes into my hair, a half-hearted apology.

Our Late Grandmother's House

A little girl stands
in the gravel drive,
a stem of wheat grass
held before her. Her
neighbors have a child
near her age, a potential
playmate. To her right
is the dense undergrowth
of Tennessee woods, new
lands and adventures.

Her mother is at the door;
her eyes through the screen
are just as measured as ours.
My sister and I speak no words
to the strangers as we pass.

I-40 Westbound, North Carolina

Traffic slows to a crawl on the highway. Inconvenienced by the pile up,

I cut in front of a semi,

confident in my vehicle's small size. Luckily, my exit is just ahead. As

the engine climbs the hill,

I catch a glimpse of red lights surrounding a milky truck in the grass,

facing me. Shards of glass

from the vision pierce my retinas. The sounds of the radio, and my voice

aiding the singer's, are whipped away,

like the passenger's breath upon impact. A fog of guilt drops over the

shattered day, and rain begins

to fall, nature's first step in cleansing the discolored flesh of the earth.

Springboro, Ohio

for Christina Bretz (Grandma Tina)

The Dairy Queen on the corner of the street we
used to walk to during those sweltering summer
                        days, now a gutted-out shell.

The idle chatter that once filled the air, consumed
by muffler engines, sputtering trucks, and blared horns.

A single tree in the front yard, which
held the little girl in its boughs, frozen in time.
                The porch swing rocks with the ghost of motion.

An empty marble tub that used to hold the sud-covered bodies
                        of gleeful children within its belly.

The plastic violin on a plastic pedestal,
              stray strings curled from neglect.

Kitchen walls lined with China plates of birds,
                  a tremor away from clipped wings.

The neighbor's walkway, still choked
           with grape ivy, philodendron, spider plants.

Gnomes across the road, posed in mocker,
                rosy cheeks and gesturing hands.

An empty bunk bed, fit for two, dust
                         its only occupant.

Dr. Robert Peters

He pokes and prods his patients, tells
them what they don't want to hear.
Try to get out and exercise, he says.
Be active. A broken record. He asks a
three-hundred-pound man, *When was the last
time you cooked your own meal, from scratch?*
The man hems and haws and avoids the question,
lamenting how busy his life is, how difficult,
stressful. The doctor nods sympathetically, thinks
of the dishes piled in the sink at home, how she
never would have allowed such disarray.

He tells the young woman later that she should refrain
from using Q-tips to clear her ears for the rest of her
life. He ignores the frown but notices a familiar stoop
in the shoulders. He signed a note excusing a boy who
had a "cold" from school that morning. The mother
hovered as the doctor wrote. Now he enters his office,
letting the nurse know he'll be with the next patient in
a few minutes. He opens a leaflet on his desk from the
funeral service yesterday, fingers the wedding ring beside it.
He glances up at the college diploma on his wall and sighs.

A Tasteful Home

In Dandridge, the olives taste black, as
the name suggests. They are dense and
split slowly, the seams opening around
the hole as I place them on my fingers,
always willing to play my alien game.

The ones in Johnson City are watery
and sour, with an aftertaste similar to
the oil. These will not fit on my fingers;
most are deflated, as if they know what
a disappointment they are. Asheville-grown

strawberries bring to mind the bruised
blackberries that sit in the bottom of a
basket, forgotten and smothered by the
weight of siblings, softened by too much
love. They taste nothing like home. There,

the strawberries are rich and voluptuous—
so red one would think the color had been
tampered with, and perhaps it had. As I sit
at the rickety table held aloft by one mediocre
leg and a few screws attached to the wall,

I smile over the fact that the taste
of local fruit is always the first
thing I miss in a new town; not
family, pets, the scenery, but
the reminiscent food of childhood.

II.

Picture it

The college girl who died when her blood sugar
dropped and her car careened off the highway,
her sister writing to the Internet for answers;

my great-grandmother who made angel food cake
taste better than I imagine even the clouds must—
her face in the casket, her red lipstick a final flirtation;

and the boy I loved when we were only children,
the stolen kiss under the dock,
the water up to our chins.
I was so nervous then.

His death a striking image. Picture it:

the ceiling
the cord, yellow,
the noose taut
the swaying

We met in elementary
school, nap time:
the floors
the mats, blue-red-blue
the hand extended
the silence.

On Identity

Let them be as flowers,
always watered, fed, guarded, admired
but harnessed to a pot of dirt.

—*Julio Noboa Polanco*

My sixth-grade English teacher points a finger at each of
us in turn, asks, "Would you rather be a flower or a weed?"

A chorus of flowers sets us off, but as the accusatory finger
moves closer, weeds begin to crop up in the familiar mouths

of classmates. When the finger of fate rests on me,
I stare at the weeds that came before and choose flower,

resolving to oppose the majority despite knowing my
answer is wrong in her eyes. Meadows filled with rolling

wildflowers that have felt no touch but the wind's can agree,
not every beauty is potted in a perfect circular home.

Abandoned Forest

Celia was mad because
I was wearing red.
She knew that I knew
they were afraid of the color,
that they would hide from it.
What she didn't know was
I wore it for that very reason.

I was confident, with my ten years,
that we wouldn't discover fairies
out in the woods behind the playground
of Dandridge Elementary.
Her father sat patiently in the car—
because fairies never reveal themselves
to anyone but children—while we
wandered through an abandoned forest.

I like to think she forgave me,
years later, when she understood
I only meant to serve as the excuse,
the reason we never found anything
but yellow honeysuckles out there.

Circumspect

She walked with her toes pointed,
as if testing the waters of life
before every step she took.

Sentries of the Cemetery

I tie a loving noose around the neck
of tree number 1427, do the same
to its brother, 1428, before stringing
my hammock between the two.
Chips of bark shower the ground
as the straps clench to hold my weight.
Cicadas sing their rebellious song while I lounge
below their home.

*   *   *

When a woodcutter finishes his labor,
he places each hour of his day in the
arms of the survivors. How strange
it is we expect trees to carry the fallen
without question. Are they bothered
by their numerical names?
Are we bothered by ours?

*   *   *

When Mother and I went to Old Gray Cemetery,
there was a separate, circular graveyard
full of identical headstones
etched with numbers and letters—
pallid alligator teeth waiting to disappear
under the mallet of a child's finger.
Only a few had names;
some were lucky enough to have wives—
someone to remember them by,

if only for a while.

*   *   *

Dusk falls, and I release the trees
from their bonds, wipe the crusted
sap from the straps.
I pat tree 1428 before I leave,
pinecones crunching like bones
                    beneath my feet.

Coccinellidae

I stare as you crawl along the shirt I tossed upon the bed that
morning, toothpick legs leaving an invisible trail of the potent
odor you emit like a skunk whenever my shadow falls across you.

This is not your house. Get out! I have catered to your needs
long enough. At first I was kind. I would return you to the
window whenever you wandered, coax you from the searing

embrace of the flower-shaped light near my bed. But it was
not long before I began to cringe at your presence. The way
you fluttered at the ceiling, bat out of hell. I stayed calm.

When you attacked I lost all coddling thoughts. You landed
on my cheek at midnight, intent on eating me, but the only
trace I could find of you on me was that ghastly smell. Now,

your corpses bob in the dirty dishes in my sink. You scuttle
along every wall, floor and ceiling, left and right. You are
even in my shoes, couch, and bed. You adorn my hair. I worry

that I will wake tomorrow to find you lining the inside of
my mouth, red inverted braces, sucking the soul from my body
with your needle feet. Next you will be in my food, and then
what will the difference be between me and you?

Pinecone

Discovered in a washing machine, no larger
than a quail egg nestled from danger.

I placed you on the desk and watched,
fascinated, as you slowly bloomed anew.

Each day your wings grew, forever
expanding, an impossible flower.

Withering Willows

She sits quietly at her desk in class,
eyes downcast, pencil held loosely in her hands,
inevitably waiting for the time to take notes.
She does not realize that her mind
is already taking notes,
picking out the smallest details
in the conversations around her.
The way the brunette dominates the discussion
in the middle of the room,
the way the boys in the corner whisper,
sneaking sly glances at the long-haired,
straight-backed girls who vomit up
the word *like* ceaselessly as they speak.

She does not want to know what they think.

Her pencil rattles against her hand,
and her leg twitches nervously.
She slides lower in her seat and
glances around, searches the faces
of strangers, the stereotyped masks of society.

Her eyes meet another girl's in the back of the room.
A smile pulls at the corners of her mouth
            and is returned.
Through the burning forest of faces,
she has found her willow tree.

Sitting in the Grass

Sensing a slight tickle on my arm,
I glance down to find a small
Lime green bug crawling along.
It maneuvers through the hairs
As if through a field.
How odd it is that I am the
Giant, the soil, the path
This kiwi bug must trod.
He circles my thumb,
And as my shadow falls—
Enacting night—he
Continues, composed
Despite my presence.

The System

I.

I show up thirty minutes late for the exam,
hair shoved into a messy bun, stray curls
escaping the embrace of the black hair tie.

I grab a Scantron and number two pencil at
the door, then walk up and accept the test
from the teacher's outstretched hand, eyes

lowered to avoid his. Finding a seat,
I stare at the paper. The teacher makes
his way to me, rests one hand

on the back of my chair, the other splayed
on the table. He leans close and whispers
he'll give me an A in the class if I make a ninety
on the test, no questions asked. All I can think

is that I have not showered in days, wonder if
he can tell. The coating of fuzz on my teeth
from a mixture of coffee, glazed donuts,

and neglect pulses in disgust at my sympathy-
worthy appearance. I glance at his face, etched
with past hardships—all the years he has lived

without his wife, the bed that is too big. A thanks
makes its way from my mouth as I bow to the task
ahead, filling empty circles with dark gray lead.

He returns to the front of the room,
confident in his stab at motivating a student.

II.

86—the number that stares up at
me after careful calculations.

Around me, fellow students are
altering the past with frantic

scribbles built on lies. I do
not possess the same reckless

nature, although I feel
the urgency as much as

they do. Two symbols
represent a third—a letter,

which determines three numbers
interrupted with a single dot

after the first that will predict
the amount of still more virtual

symbols that I will receive in
the form of collateral for being

a *promising student.* Resisting the
urge to cave to the twitch in my

fingers, I let my pencil clatter to
the table and hand the teacher the

paper with my future on it.
He glances at it, then wraps

an arm around my shoulder,
presses me to his side, and

plants a sloppy kiss on my
forehead. he tells me, *you'll*

be fine. He was right—between
his hand and the official records,

the numbers changed. He told me that day
to make sure I come back and see him.

                                    I never have.

Counterfeit Manifestation

I hand you the paper, the mask
of indifference daintily yet
securely smoothed over my face.

My eyes watch yours as
they skim over the words,
lips moving silently as you
take them in. You finish,
give a curt nod, return it to
my hands and say, "It's good."

Those words—so simple—
so often spoken, become
the universe in an instant,
but the mask is firmly in place.

Laugh of the Hyena

He follows behind as I walk past,
stalking like a hyena as I make my
way to another part of the hallway.
I sit on the floor as he stops, above
and behind me, stares blankly at a
                          poster on the wall.

He accosts me with his nonsensical
laughter, monologuing to the air—
the kind of man who speaks in order
to be heard, no respect for the power
of words, the grace that comes with
                          wielding them. I open a book.

Behind me, he pauses, glares at
the poster, hand on chin, begging
to be asked what he thinks. I ignore
my cue, let the moment pass, yet still
he stands, waits until the sigh, the glance
                          over, and the noise begins anew.

The Stick Man's Sculpture

—Stout Drive Circle, East Tennessee State University

It is constructed as if a bird's nest
had toppled, with you inside.

I gaze at the latticed saplings,
arranged with care by diligent hands—

over a hundred volunteers,
three weeks in early November.

What other Easter eggs has
the Stick Man left in his shadow—

Chapel Hill, France,
Korea, stops in between.

It is said he gathered stray
sticks while they worked,

a tireless mother assembling her nest
with each carefully chosen rod.

Nothing But Words

But what does it mean?
a persistent peer asked.
She sat leaning forward
in her seat, as if she could
reach out a hand and pull
the answer from his mind
with nothing but brute
determination. His mouth
opened like a hidden tunnel
suddenly revealed before
blending back into the foliage.
He turned his gaze to the paper,
forcing himself to face the words
he had written on the page.

Greystone Heights Road, Gatlinburg

—December 2016

At one house the front driveway was perfectly intact.
Two rocking chairs stood at the entrance. One new,
the other charred in the back, secure in the base.

The perfect chair tilted toward its wounded sister,
left arm resting over the right of the injured
as if to offer comfort,
twin elders whispering what they saw.

To the left, a spiral staircase,
singed black to brown to yellow to white,
each swirl a different color, a different bruise.

Outside, where the garage doors used to be,
was a stone cherub, its back to the road—
stark white against the black and gray,
its childish curls suspended in the breeze.

Picture of a Man

I could almost see him
with one of those pitchforks,
not a violent image, but more
akin to the classic picture of the
farmer and his wife. In that photo,
the man seems reserved. This man
looks more accepting. He's had that
pitchfork for years, and he knows he'll
never do anything else. He's seen the
power his weapon can yield, all the
work he could get done in a year.

But he lacks motivation, agency.
He does not care if his fingers
stiffen around the handle, molding
like clay to the instrument—
no longer an independent entity,
merely a farmer with a pitchfork.

Damaging the Sundial

My sisters and I measured our childhood by the four trees
in front of our house. There were years when the trees were
young and in need of a helpful stake to stand tall and straight,

the years when their shadows foretold the seasons against
the stone pyramid that stood at the center like a sundial, the years
when the breeze blew new color clockwise across their leaves.

Those days, everyone we knew was solid and reliable. Aunts
and uncles visited often, and Grandfather chased us girls
through the yard with a squirt gun bloated with water.

Then came the year one tree was struck by lighting
in the night; no one saw the accident,
just the massive trunk in the grass the next morning.

Our great-grandmother fell at 89
and was placed in a nursing home.
Our four seasons became three.

The second tree was consumed by a quiet disease—
termites, who had migrated from the husk
of the dead tree, or so we presumed.

By this time, the oldest of us three sisters had moved,
not unlike the termites, to occupy the husk of great-
grandma's house on the hill behind ours.

The charred tree was exorcised.
Grandfather had his first knee surgery.
And so we were down to two trees.

The seasons fell out of sync. When I left for university,
I was not sure if there were still two trees, or if only
one remained loyal to the dust of its compatriots.

Great-Grandma passed, my younger sister
followed me to university, and Grandfather
had several more surgeries on his knee.

When I saw him that summer, the scars across the cap
of his knee mirrored the painful cuts of age in the last tree,
deep reddish-black slashes that glistened in the sun.

For the Girl Across the Way Admiring a Flower

She stands on the sidewalk,
oblivious to the bustle around her.
Her long purple dress brushes the ground,
sweeps autumn leaves under its folds.

Her hand is raised as if to cup the flower
above her, yet she does not touch it.
The palm withdraws, and she preserves
the flower with the flash of her phone.

I stand across the street, wonder briefly
if I've been caught in the background.
She lowers the phone and straightens the
hijab with those careful fingers. I smile as she
walks on, leaving no trace of her presence.

My College Roommate's Graduation Day, 2019

Your uncle looked at me
like I was terror
come to your door,

dripping on the steps.
No one could be bothered
to fetch a towel,
venture, *how are you?*

I stood at the entry,
facing the young boy—
your cousin—whose voice
was high in fright or excitement
I could not tell.

Abby didi, you're all wet.

The room, full of your relatives;
your cousin—this boy,
the rest—I don't know.

This is my home, too;
why doesn't it feel like it?

Lightning cracks the sky,
the boom immediate, resonating.

I feel the tug of water on my limbs
like this boy who wants
something from me,

but what, I cannot tell—
playmate, friend, new relative?

Too exhausted to ask,
I close the door softly,
turn back to the stairs

leading down, away
from this house
which is no longer mine.

Mirror Perceptions

I.

The author of the ballerina book asks me why I'm here, at this
internship.
I tell her I want to be a book editor, that this is good practice.

She nods, agrees, asks me where I plan on getting a job. *Nashville,*
I say,
because it's the closest city to home that has a Simon & Schuster.

She's been to Nashville. She says it's sort of depressing—a lot of
women with
guitars on street corners, hoping to be discovered—the next Taylor
Swift.

II.

At the fundraiser, an old woman comes in, the mother-in-law of
one of the authors. She
sits in a chair across from me and a little to the right. We make eye
contact and she winks.

The publisher, my boss, leans in next to me and whispers the
woman is a psychic. I don't
know how much I believe in psychics, but I do believe I want to get
to know this one.

Later, after the food is served, she sits beside me, asks that question again, why am I here? I tell her what I tell everyone. She smiles. *I was hoping you'd say something in the music industry.*

My head tilts to the right, thrown off by her reply. *I only ask,* she says, *because when I saw you across the room earlier, you had music notes above your head.*

The whites of my eyes expand in the reflection of her glasses. I've always loved music.
I could be a singer, I think, yet all I can picture are lonely women with even lonelier guitars

sitting on unforgiving brick steps outside glass buildings, their image distorted in the windows of skyscrapers. OBJECTS IN MIR-ROR ARE LARGER THAN THEY APPEAR.

III.

The food is gone, the wine supply is dwindling. The old woman stands to leave, gives me
a final farewell wink. She tells me she looks forward to hearing my music.

I wish I could go with her, hope that I see her again. As the glass door closes behind her, I realize, OBJECTS IN MIRROR ARE CLOSER THAN THEY APPEAR, not LARGER.

On a Military Helicopter Passing Overhead

leaves spring
from trees
en masse,
soldiers
without
parachutes

My Boss's Husband

He waved to her with his wrist just under his chin,
fingers wriggling like tadpoles as he stood at the window.
He worried over the hanging plants, then came inside
the bookstore. The top two buttons of his dress shirt
were open—the bottom one too, which exposed his soft,
round stomach, so perfectly circular, as if a child were
curled inside, nestled under his silver dew chest curls.

His hair was always wild from the hours he spent in windy fields,
testing the airplanes he made for a living. She was proud of his
mechanical mind; she often told me about the airplanes he made.
He carried a pipe, which he mumbled around expertly. Often,
to remind her to eat, he stopped by the store during lunch,
brought her soup or garlic knots from the restaurant next door.

She welcomed him as a child would her father, with arms thrown
wide,
desperate to be grasped gently round the waist and lifted into the
tobacco embrace.
Yet he would not lift with his tadpole fingers, but stood rigid and
awkward
until she pulled away. He told her the hanging plants needed
water,
then handed her the food and a flower clipped from his garden.

He brought me one once—a flower, that is. I pretended not to
hear as he showed her
her flower, then asked her in a whisper if I would like one too. I
could picture
her nodding behind my back as she took his shoulders and

steered him toward me.
She may have given him a little push as well, the same way a mother
encourages her son when she wants him to make friends.

The base of the flower was wrapped in a wet paper towel, and the thorns
were trimmed like a cat's claws, missing the barbed tips. Such care.
I envied them their simple love. Theirs was an intimacy outside the physical,
one that bloomed from careful observations and quiet tenderness.
They were both in their seventies, yet I knew they were still children,
younger even than I was with my two meagre decades.

Ascent to Pandemonium

The breath clings to my windpipe, scraping
its way up and out of my esophagus.

There is a demon in my throat, acting up
every time I attempt to swallow.

He expands to block the air
from entering the lungs.

I attack his house, a feeble
tornado, but he is in the eye,

calm in the midst of my storm.
This is the worst sickness of all.

I climb to the top of the stairs,
force my body into overexertion,

my heart beating *you are fine
you are fine* into my head.

III.

Vital Dance

In bed, listening to the metronome in my ear, the tiny timekeeper
who will not let me sleep, taking life with each beat into the
drum,

      tap by tap, a Morse code message in a long-lost language.

Why do I sleep knowing that time will pass as I do so? I am free
to dance
when Father Time is drowsy, lulled by the white coin in the sky,
suspended

      between heads or tails. In those moments, we wait, hold

our breath, and dance together in familiarity from which we
came and
shall return one day, when our knees are weak and our hair a
color

      akin to the moon.

One two *heads* three four *tails* five six *last* seven eight *day*

      hush

Snippets—I Can't

"Sometimes I can't tell if I like a girl
        as a friend or as girlfriend material."

Snippets of a conversation overheard
        in passing while boarding the subway.

Sometimes I can't tell whether
        I speak aloud or in my paper-thin head.

It does not help that things
        echo here in the chambers of Manhattan.

I can't tell if I can hear
        correctly, if I can see the faces correctly.

Sometimes I think I see
        myself. Material becomes immaterial

like a chain of paper angels, wings
        severed with each gentle snip of the doors.

Uprooted

Bees climb blindly into my cocoon,
confused by this man-made thing that
does not belong, a horizontal tree
that opens and closes, foreign Venus flytrap.

I wriggle in the depths, adjust my shape,
press my face against the fibers. They
leave no marks on me, yet I still feel the
imprint long after I've packed up and left.

I hold hands with the willow, run my
fingers through those of my savior,
thanking the being that keeps me
from falling to the ground.

Ants crawl over my sandaled feet
while the wind pulls the hand from
mine; we drop our branches, allow
gravity to separate us once again.

The Fall of Eve

They stood together at the top of the stairs.
She gazed down the flight before them as if
to receive an attendant who would ask for
their tickets. He probed her mind, saw that
she was imagining a red apple falling down
the stairs, jagged slices and bruises opening
on the tender flesh. It rolled to rest at the base
of the descent. She wondered how long it would
take before someone cared to pick it up, if he
would throw it away or bring it close to his face
and breathe in the smell to determine its worth.
Perhaps he would place it where it could live out its
days watching the motion picture reel by as it turned
brown from the inside out, or maybe it would remain
in the vacant corner at the bottom, forgotten despite
its glorious fall—a trail of ants thirsty for its sweet tears
                          the only sign of a skirmish.

How It Could Have Happened

"What's your name?"

                      "Claire."

"Claire," he repeats.

My name always sounded flat to me,
but when he says it, he lingers
on the vowel, drawing
                  out the "air."

It's eerie, this feeling.

We stand in the middle of the double
entrance to the Knoxville Public Library;
two people, one coming—
                  one going.

"Where are you from, Claire?"

                  "It's—" I pause, unsure
how to evade the question.
        "It's a ways away from here.
        You probably don't know the place."

"I know a lot of places."

He smiles,
        sticks his hands in his pockets.

The circulation librarian is watching us
                                        through the glass door.

I can't stop glancing at her.

"How far away is it?"

My eyes are pulled back to his face.

                            "Oh, about an hour and a half," I say,
                            sure the information is useless.

There are a lot of places an hour
and a half away from where we stand.

I inch closer to the second set of doors,
                            which lead outside.

"We're friends, right?" he asks.

I nod, my gaze on the door,
        hands clenched to hide the tremble.

                            I force my fists to unravel.
                            "Sure. We're friends, I guess."
I look at him.
        He smiles again.

His teeth are thin and yellow, like a rat's.
They look brittle, as if they could fall out.

"I have a lot of friends who are girls.
I met them the same way I met you

                            just now.

You should come over sometime—

to my place, meet them. We can all
       be friends
              and have a good time, together."

I don't respond.

I put my hand on the outer door,
              angle my body away from him.

The librarian is standing now, watching.

The man on display with me
does not appear to notice our viewers.

He moves closer.

"What are you doing right now?" he asks.

His voice is low. He is bent slightly at the waist,
leaning his shoulders and face closer.

"Do you want to go with me to meet them?"

         Them. His friends.

He lifts his hand as if to touch my face.

               "I'm sorry,"
I stammer.
               "I have to go."

I push open the door,
feel the rush of air and noise—
       loud as the blood roaring in my ears.

I look back to see him shake his head, turn away.

I nearly trip down the concrete steps.
At my car, the books—
thrown in the passenger seat.
I climb in and lock the doors.
Grip the steering
wheel—
not so hard.

Breathe.

*　　*　　*

I'm not unnerved by what he said,
but by how easy
he made it seem.

I could have left with him—
disappeared—
a simple thing, really.

A Delicate Gift

She unspools the
bow of the ribbon.
Her hands shake,
pulling it taut.
An accident.
It snaps at her,
nonetheless.
Then she eases her
finger under the tape,
cringes every time
she hears a tear—
A glance at
his face
and a soft smile.

Viola da Gamba

It is difficult to learn the craft
from an invisible instructor;
he cannot see the fingers of the musician's left hand
press the strings into the polished instrumental wood.
The bow sways through the air,
nips the taut strings in passing,
the underbelly of an invisible ship
clapping against the swell of waves.
The student has yet to grasp the language of this dance.
There, on the tip of his tongue,
a flicker of the word glides
succinct between the masts,
the wire strings at the tips of the master's fingers.
The amateur tries to keep up, make chase,
but he is too foreign, clumsy.
Hairs begin to tangle.
Caught, he panics, tilts;
the song of the instructor continues without pause.

Song of Habit

Her fingers play piano keys across her leg.
She looks like a piano herself—
white blouse, black skirt over thin black leggings.
The whites of her fingers flash across her calf.
Sometimes the tempo in her head
seems to be trailing, skin gliding across skin.
Other times it is the beat of a metronome,
each hard, soundless tap
knocks around the heads of onlookers.
She notices the eyes.
All on her.
The dead skin of a finger
catches in the fabric of her leggings.

Excerpts from a Dream Journal

I.

The girl is always suspended in flight a few
feet above the heads of those she is leading—
children, teenagers, the young and injured. She
wears a simple white nightgown with lace trim.
It has clear buttons up the collar that button
nothing; they're purely ornamental.

The children are dressed as if marching to a riot,
or as if they had just come from one. Behind
each child's heel rises a cloud of dust, suspended—
like the girl—in the air. From the front, each child
appears to be tumbling, impatient, into the one
before him. It looks as if they are moving, yet
I know, somehow, they are not. They look
like a revolving background in an old film.

They are headed somewhere important.
Something big is happening. I know it,
but I cannot follow. I can only watch
the picture of them rotate. On occasion,
the girl in lace trim will lower, then ascend,
drifting as a kite does on the currents.
I had this same dream many times as a child.

II.

There is a vast warehouse filled with oversized
crates and sky-high metal shelves. I am always

alone at first, browsing the antiques on the shelves.
Sometimes I find items I owned, ones I knew
were in my room, where I am sleeping, dreaming.
I find the pink diary with the white cat on it
from fifth grade and the unicorn statue
with the luscious magenta mane who kept
guard on my bookshelf for years.

After I find the items, the man appears, always
with a gun, and tells me to go with him.
I run instead. There are gunshots.
I climb a metal shelf, look down at the man.
I spend days running from him in my dreams.
I do not know who he is or what he wants,
but each night he is there amidst the antiques,
hunting for the single item he desires to keep.

III.

I stand outside Swann's Chapel Church,
watch as a school bus dives into a pond
and is swallowed. I look for the bus,
yet it is gone, along with the pond.
I plunge my hands into the soil,
searching. The earth is soft and malleable,
and my hands emerge with empty water bottles.

I pull the bottles, drained of their purpose,
from the soil until there is a tower of plastic,
waste, behind me, and no water in sight.
The only dew that remains clings to the grass
I search through, unsure what it is I am seeking.

The Big Texan Steak Ranch

The daughter had just started her period,
so she wore loose blue pajama pants
on the way home from Colorado,
headed to Tennessee. They stopped
in Texas to eat at The Big Texan.
The mother was a fan of Barbara Streisand,
who shot a clip from *The Guilt Trip* at the restaurant.

The place was like a giant prison mess hall.
The other diners were fellow prisoners.
The deer and buffalo that lined the walls with
their unblinking glass eyes were the guards.
When she got up to use the restroom,
the animal eyes of the dead and the living
traced her path through the wooden tables.
Perhaps they could smell the freshness of it on her.

Palm Up, Fingers Curled
(Or, This Is How It Happened)

I sit on my grandparent's back porch,
   in a chair at their glass table.

Grandpa is on my left;
my father across from him,
to the right of me at the head of the table.

Grandpa is describing the recent
        abduction of a young woman.

It had been in the news a few days before.

My father had yet to hear the story—
it wasn't just an abduction, we learned;

two men had kidnapped, raped, mutilated,
        then murdered the woman.

Grandfather goes into specifics,
       describing how the men had
       tied her to the bedpost
and taken turns.

The young woman was young,
a girl really, just sixteen years old.

Grandpa makes eye contact with me—
then with his son
      as he relays the most gruesome details.

At other times during the telling,
he looks down and speaks to his
reflection in the dusty glass of the table.

His face, at those moments, has a look of incredulity,
as if even he is shocked to hear the story he is voicing.

My father breathes the word "Jesus"
at various intervals. He glances at me,

                                on occasion.

The things he must be imagining—
worst-case scenarios involving me

                        in her place.

When I first sat down
I had not known what they were discussing.

It was summer, early July.

Our entire family was over
for our annual cookout.

I had expected the conversation to be light, airy,
like biting into a slice of watermelon.

                Instead, I sit down to hear him say
one of the men had cut off the young woman's left breast.

And I don't just mean her nipple, he said.
                                Her entire breast.

He holds his hand out, palm up with his fingers curled,
as if that very breast was perched there in his hand.

The air around us grows oppressive.

I do not want to stay—to listen—
but I also don't want to stand

                                and leave so soon after having
            just sat down.

So I stay. I listen.

Until my grandfather
                holds out that hand,

his palm a sign of wealth—
        all the years he has lived

                    weaving a tangled tapestry
                      across his soft, tan skin;

the shape his palm makes, as if he were offering
        his beating heart,
                or if his other hand joins in,
                    as if he were begging for mercy—

but it is just the one hand,
        golden band reflecting the sun's gaze.
                              I look away.

crimson thoughts

my hands are *red red red*

can't be mine

remember the gravel in my palms,
the *shushing* of my hands across pavement.

remember seeing the work boots
behind me, my neck craned to see.

remember the train as it passed,
sound without savior.

not remembering what happened next,
how I got home.

not remembering whose blood is
hidden in the crevices of this body.

can't be mine

all I see is *red red red*

0.6 inches

I.

Our golden retriever died
                on the carpet in our living room.

She lay stretched out on her side. We placed
                water by her head. She did not drink.

I lay next to her, my face mirrored in her eyes.
                She whimpered. I stroked her oily fur.

For days we maneuvered around her body. Surrendering—
                finally—we brought her to the vet.

             *   *   *

Years later, our feline birthed a litter
                on the same carpet—four kittens.

The next yielded double. We had her fixed after
                that, though the vet said she was already pregnant

again.

             *   *   *

We raised another golden, a girl
                fixed as soon as she was of age.

She watched the birth of the kittens

with the keen eye of a midwife

and licked each one clean as if it were her own.

II.

I think of how our golden retriever would
　　　　　　have been an excellent mother.

I think of our role as superiors,
　　　　　　our decisions shaping their lives.

*　　*　　*

I lay awake at night

rubbing the skin between the nail and
　　　　　　first crease of my finger,

a surface larger than the size of a developing kitten
　　　　　　in its mother's womb, unaware

how sterile—cold—life can be;
　　　　　　safe in its dark, watery love chamber.

Prisoner

He is there again—
on the doorstep.
His car idles at the edge
of the walkway, the side
mirror inches from the mailbox
with the words *Jim & Carol*
scrolled across its face in an elegant
form of calligraphy not unlike a wedding invitation.

He shifts the warm pizza box
from one palm to the other,
glances up. She snaps the metallic
blinds closed, retreats into the darkness.

Downstairs, she hears footsteps
trace the familiar path to the door.
Voices are heard, a burst of sudden,
strained laughter. Her hand flies to her mouth
when the car door slams. She returns
to the window as the engine revs, snakes
a few fingers through the blinds again
only to see the distant red flash of the
taillights as the delivery vehicle turns the corner.

I Am

I am a wife,
youthful and perfect
like a Covergirl
if the Covergirl
was the girl next door
who you always say
could be one if only she
tried, if only she put in
just a little more effort.

I am a ripe
pair of breasts
served up on a platter,
bright and perky,
never wilting,
like the endless
dream in your mind,
like the woman
you saw on the subway
that one time, glimpsed
in profile on the car
you just got off,
forever haunting your
sleep with the possibilities.

I am my husband
living in technicolor,
always confused,
disoriented, vaguely
turned on, always

up for the *idea*
of a good time,
never willing to commit.

I am my husband,
and I do not see my wife,
could not tell you
where she's wandered.
I am my husband,
and I see you when
I'm in the mood,
think of you when
it's convenient.
I am my wife
and I do not know
where she has gone.
     Can you help me find her?
Her face is . . .
    like my desire
when it's two in the morning
and she is asleep beside me,
dead to my wants and needs,
beautiful in that unattainable
way that drives you mad
enough to maybe preserve
her body just as it is,
veiled in shadows,
like when you try to picture
your mother as a young woman,
a being entirely separate from you.

My Time

Shadows quiver on the wall
as the candle flickers, then
fizzles to nothing. The hands
creep along, comfortably
concealed within the night.
I know there is no hope left,
no chance of survival. All I
can do is close my eyes and
concentrate on my breath.

I shouldn't be this terrified.
They warned me he would
come. In my passion, I ignored
their incessant voices. I close
my eyes in dreaded anticipation as the
cold fingers tease their way up my spine
in their own twisted anticipation. Still,
I can't help but think, It was worth it.

The Scale of the World

I.

A round belly used to represent luck—
now, jutting pelvises and collar bones
are how we judge our worth.

II.

Cattle dine more frequently than some
children, while other kids eat everything
in sight only to lie in bed loathing themselves.

III.

Sugar reigns from conveyor
belts while apples turn
soft on the shelf.

IV.

Chickens stare through mesh sunglasses
while the ignorant cries of a pig pierce the
air, trusting the man in the crimson boots
even as he opens a river on its neck.

Return to the Womb

Under the covered porch, drops
ping off the aluminum roof.
Rain learning the language,
altering its course, now a slant.
She sits, seduced by the water's lullaby.

shush *patter-patter* *shush*

Dance of seduction: the grass—
taunting, enticing—
swish *patter-patter*
shimmering in the misty morning.

Images, fantasies:
mud squelching between toes,
diving feet-first into a black mirror,
pleasant chills—temptation.

shush *patter-patter* *shush*

Slender clouds drifting inches above dense water,
the woman rendered a child again,
lost below the water's surface;
if heaven had cars, this is what it would look like—
parade of colorless cotton candy.

She, woman-child, pictures dark fingers
snaking through the water,
sucking the treat from her vision as her eyes blur—
fantasies of heaven followed by fantasies of hell.

shush   *patter-PATTER*

Pounding rain, now—
serious as a tsunami.
How quickly the tides turn.
She curls, fetal, against the chair—
drowning in her self—
the only sound a dull, watery roar.

The Influence of Brian Crain

She sits on the inky couch,
cross-legged and hunched
over, struggling to make the
words flow. She pauses, becomes
aware of the stifling silence. With
a laugh, she reaches for her phone.
The "Butterfly Waltz" begins to emit
from the depths of the device, and
the cogs whirl into motion. Like the
dancer in a music box, she cannot
function without the accompanying
tune. Her hands glide over the keyboard,
transform into peach flats, ribbons laced
up the legs of her fingers. Together they
work to translate the music into images,
the images to ideas, ideas to words,
and words to a story—the story of the
hunchbacked ballerina.

Sown Woman

She keeps all her secrets
hidden inside like a bouquet,
and when someone inquires
about her heart, she will
gladly give an Easter lily
imprinted with the name
of her childhood friend,
a daisy deflowered by
all that could have been—
a dandelion that carries with it
all of the wishes she has ever made.
And little by little
her bouquet will dwindle.
Although she will
be lost to the wind,
she will have spread her
garden of memories
across as many lifetimes
as there are seeds
in a pomegranate.

IV.

Inked

He wasn't born with a book
in his hands—but his heart—and
every day the paper cut deeper
until someone noticed the blood
on his shirt. She gave him a quill
and said, "You must let the world
share in your sorrows. It will provide
the gauze and you the anesthesia."

Molded Earth

The way he softens his voice
when he speaks to her and no
one else, knowing others have
not offered the same courtesy.

A woman who smiles at each soul
she passes, even though she was
told it is a bad idea, that it
gives the wrong impression.

The boy who serenades the
girl on the swing set beside
him with his favorite love song.

The child who claims
the squirrel in the road
is not dead, only sleeping—

like the monster formed by piling people on people,
they bind together, become one solitary figure, alone
in the clay belly, open mouth filled with the dirty
soil of smothered deeds and staunched blood.

Base Hospital Nurse

You swathe me in blankets,
bring biscuits and corned beef,
rest a cold rag on my forehead,
and check regularly to make
sure it's still damp.

You sit by the bed;
we talk of nothing as
you exhume the toxins
from me, draw them
into you through the
movement of your
hands, your voice—
a gentle general who
has yet to lose a soldier.

Morsels from the Vine

The piercing scream of the wheel on the shopping cart
makes the woman flinch as she pushes it over to the produce
section. Her son giggles in the seat in front of her, his thin
feet dancing through the holes of his cage. She picks up a
bag of grapes and places it beside the boy. The sound of the
zipped seal unzipping reverberates off the walls. She winces
and glances around before reaching her hand into the opening.
Pulling out a bundle, she moves the cart forward again, realizing
she's been stationary for too long. She browses through the store,
shelves lined with impossible temptations, feeding him grapes
all the while. He arches his neck, a baby bird impatient for
food that has already been devoured, blindly stealing it from
his mother's stomach. When the bag is half empty, she parks
the cart filled with miscellaneous items in a deserted aisle,
folds her son to her chest, and flies from the scavenged lot.

Nursery Rhyme

For the most part, the poem
runs free on the page, but
every once in a while, there
is a childish interruption—
look at me, look at me!
I am special.

Although childish, it has
the power of an anchor; it
grounds attention to the
familiar, arrests the harsh
world—reminding us of fairies
and people who live in oversized
shoes—glass slippers, golden hair,

symbols of hope, dreams. Is not the
world but an illusion, mundane
interposed with the occasional
sighting of reality, magic?
The empty crib sways in answer.

Slight Death on a Forest Bench

A tiny, near-translucent spider
tidies her home on the bench
as I watch beside her. Behind
us, a large copper salamander
slithers through the leaves
as a second spider, black,
creeps to devour the first
in her own home.
The salamander
does not pause,
nor do I, yet
I write this
small poem.

Reticent

The stranger who lends an extra
five for diapers at the grocery store.

A mother kissing a boy's scraped
knee after a bicycle wreck.

On the side of the road, a man who
insists on feeding his dog before himself.

A nurse who turns on the television at five
sharp each day, knowing it soothes the patients.

The little boy who writes a note of appreciation
for his teacher, earning her a thousand dollars.

A patron who leaves a tip large
enough to pay the waiter's rent.

The young woman who smiles at the boy meandering past,
head down, hands shoved in blue cotton fabric, kicking stones.

The Essence of Lounging

Security is a kind of death.

—*Tennessee Williams*

She relished the firmness
Of the soil against her back,
The pressure of gravity
Pinning her to the earth—
Like a fly caught in a web,
A solid part of *terra firma*.
Perhaps when she finally
Decides to rise, when the
Spider eventually comes,
Her body will have left an
Indentation—a memory
Of what has been.

The Art of Creation

A boy stands on a street corner in Paris,
watches the man across the way paint a
fresh view with each calculated stroke
of the brush. A wisp of a child observes
her grandmother as she weaves the story
of today into the tapestry. A young man
in the decrepit library of a college, the
sun illuminating the book in his hand.

A dropped coin in an empty guitar case,
bodies at an art show. A photographer
who captures graffiti, displays it,
blue-thumbed amplification. Worn
records, converted VHS tapes, dusty
memories undusted by tender hands.

Golden Droplet

He noticed it in her hair one day
as they were talking in the empty
hall. He pointed it out, a yellow
contrast in the auburn, like fall.

She had blushed and untangled
it from the smooth curtain, thanked
him for noticing. He smiled as
she glanced around for a trash

can and presented his hand, said
he would throw it away for her.
Holding the flower between two
fingers, she dropped in into his palm.

He remembered being disappointed
that her hand hadn't brushed his.
When she wasn't looking, he placed
the bright blossom in his pocket.

It sits on his windowsill,
now a dry, colorless husk.

Concrete Ardor

At an art gallery, she'll talk of random objects and
images she sees in the abstract paintings, like animals
in the sky. Can you see them? she points. On a hiking
trail in Asheville, one of the ones with signposts that read
this tree used to be carved by American Indians to make
spoons, this one, bowls. She skips from one post to the next,
leans forward with her hands clasped behind her back,
bouncing excitedly on her heels all the while.

Somewhere you can watch her eyes go wide in wonder
as she takes in all the miracles of life around her—
like a newborn baby who is now old enough to see the
world beyond her mother's smiling face for the first time.

A Regulated Man

He laughed as if he'd lived his entire
life in a library, trained to contain that
impulsive explosion of joy. He managed
to shape something sudden and wild,
and she loved him for it.

The Proust Phenomenon

The pages wave at her as she
glances through the book. A few
over-exuberant leaves nip her nose
when she leans in. She scrunches up
her face with a laugh and touches a
finger to the injury. Pulling back, she
tsk-tsks, reprimanding the stray
spirits. She presses her nose as close
to the stitching of the open novel as
she can, breathes in the familiar smell
of knowledge—crayon boxes and dusty
library shelves, the lingering vanilla
perfume of the previous owner.

Lying on her stomach at the beach,
legs crossed behind her, shiny from
the sunscreen bottle with the image
of the blond little girl, finger on cheek,
the mischievous brown dog intent on
making off with her blue bottoms.

Suspended between two trees
in a hammock at school, head
cradled in her arm, the open
book refracting the sunlight as
petals fall into the oversized net.

Sitting in the doctor's
office, bent almost double,
staring at the blurred words

in an attempt to suppress
the sounds around her.

The pages continue to rustle in
her hands, knowing they have
found a worthy reader—one who
seeks to pump life into the worlds
of the dead, placing an invisible
snapshot of her day like a bookmark
into the pages of every story she's
read, a scattered photo album.

Master of the Galaxy

A basketball player, tossing and spinning
the planets in the air, twirling, throwing them
above his head, behind his back. He rotates
one on a single finger, pulls it close and
slows it down for a
moment,
suspending time.

He smiles, runs a finger along one of the lines—
black ribbon racing across the world. He pulls back,
resumes his circus act,
spinning and tossing and twirling and risking it all—
a single ball,
sphere of orange and black.

V.

Timelapse

I loved swimming as a child.
The way you would lap me up,
twirl me around and nudge me
back to the surface. You knew
I didn't belong there, but I gasped
a breath of air before sinking back
into your sun-kissed embrace,
oblivious to the danger.

Now you are angry with me.
You foam and seethe, and
even my salty tears betray me,
mingling with their brethren.
My body is mostly water.
You, the sea, know this—
I can feel you seeping through
my nose, my ears, my eyes, my eyes.

I am drowning in my own malleable
fluids, but I blame you, my childhood
friend. And I blame the moon, who
is so greedy to swallow me up.

Decrepit Motor Home

I stand in the small shower,
Victorian wallpaper to my
right, a plastic guard rail and
curtain that blocks nothing, not
even the water, which seeps
beneath the uneven gap between
it and the tub, to my left.

Lukewarm water teases
me for a moment before
switching to ice that drags
shudders from my
vulnerable body.

A spider decides this is the
opportune moment to introduce
himself. He hangs from the bar,
retreats whenever I straighten.

I exit the space feeling more soiled
than when I entered. The oils from
the conditioner cling to the tangled
locks at the back of my head.

Opening the door, I leave one small
space only to enter another, slightly
larger—a fun house mirror room that
throws unsightly parts of my body
back at me from every angle.

I wrap myself in the cerulean beach
towel; the whites of my knuckles
holding the fabric in place reflect
across each mirror, one final taunt
before our next scheduled encounter.

Fishing Lessons

I caught one, my sister says, reeling in the line. Her pole
curves toward the water, its spine arching like a frightened
cat's. The handle is snug against her hip, and the weight of
her body rests solely on her haunches as she leans back,
mirroring the pole. The line sings, moving faster than the eye
can catch, and the smooth surface of the water breaks, spits

a bass out of its dark maw, spattering the deck with flecks of
water and blood. She swings her pole first right, then left,
displaying her catch. Mother digs in the tackle box for the
pliers while my older sister and I gather around the victor,
congratulating her on a job well done, when the bass lets
out a shudder, releasing a waterfall of embryos onto the deck.

My sister and I jump backward, unsure what is happening.
She's just laid her eggs, says Mother. *She thinks she's going to die.*
We push the eggs into the water with our flip-flopped feet,
being as gentle as we can. We know they will not survive.
Mother unhooks the hollowed fish, tossing it back to the
depths. It lands with a resounding splash, taking with it all

our oxygen. Hunched in our lawn chairs on the deck,
staring at the dark spots on the wood where the eggs had
been, we turn our collective gaze out over Douglas Lake
from the edge of our grandparent's *T*-shaped dock.

Dear Grandpa Sawyer,

John caught a trout today—his first.
I watched from the top of the hill as
he reeled it in, and let me tell you,
that boy's sure got some strength in
him. I thought that fish was going to
pull him in for a swim instead of the
other way around. It was so huge he
had to drag it through the mud on the
bank, which squelched and sucked in
protest, refusing to relinquish one of its
prized children. I've got a picture that I'll
put in here. John says he wants you to frame
it and send him that dime you've promised him.

Yours,
Amelia Gene

The Flood

Once, the lake was over-watered;
it stretched like a cat into yards,

rubbed against back porches, made
docks strain like dogs at their leash.

My two sisters and I
wadded through grass

as pleasurable as silk
against our calloused soles.

We climbed atop the picnic table
bobbing in the water

and into the branches of the tree above.
There, we pretended we'd been stranded,

perching on limbs like herons.
I rested low in the tree, let my legs

embrace the water, felt the liquid
brush of a bluegill's greeting,

its excitement moving, electric, up my leg.

Uncle Kracker's "Follow Me"

She is in the shower when
the song comes on. She
reaches out for the white wall,
shoulder against the wet plastic,
the palm of one hand pressed to
starkness, reaching for the ocher
face that is no longer there.

The noise escapes her lips,
and she is grateful for the
waterfall above her head,
pounding the sounds against
the ground of the tub. The
words of the singer circle
her mind with memories.

She sinks to the floor,
arms pulling bare legs to
chest as the steam rises
to obscure her outline.

Mother, Sister, and I Hunt Ghost Crabs on the Florida Shore

We came armed with small plastic butterfly nets—
one was orange, another purple, with butterflies inlaid
in the handle. We brought flashlights and a single blue
bucket; the bucket was to be the cage—a net, the roof.

True to their name, the crabs were only visible
when they glided into the path of a flashlight.
They ran, greeted on the east by yelps
and the smack of a net against broken shells;
to the west were the gentle, rhythmic waves.
Once our bucket was filled with their light thumps
and soft clicks, we headed back to the hotel.

They escaped en route, scuttled under a door
on the first floor of our hotel. We did not knock
or warn whoever lived beyond the threshold,
but set the bucket down and ghosted up the stairs,
convinced shrieks would follow, but there were none.

Rainelle, West Virginia

—Appalachia Service Project Volunteer Site

We use water-resistant paint
on the concrete stilts;
the house is perched above,
climbing from the flood
that destroyed its shadow.
One set of stilts supports air alone
while the owner lives in a tent nearby.
We are quiet as we paint his.

It rained many times in the week
we were there. We were told
the locals fear the rain.
Most importantly, they told us
the people here are not victims—
we were never to use that word.

Trout Fishing

She sits across from him at the small coffee shop,
gazes out the window speckled with rain.
She can see their reflections—the sudden,
sharp fish hook of her jaw, his long fingers
curled around the saucer of coffee between them—
so many things that can snare a person.

He looks at her, notices the soft seams of her sweater,
how the wide neck leaves ample room for her to maneuver,
snug and free as the trout that slipped away from his fine hook
last summer at Watauga Lake. The sudden glint of steel
off sunlight, the slight jerk of his hand on the rod in anticipation.
He could feel the hook claw harmless at the scales even then.

Nocturnal Auras

A blue trail of bright noctiluca in the
waves, river through the ocean.
Fireflies pulse in the fading light,
absorb the last rays of sun.
The candle flickers at the log cabin
window, conducted by invisible hands.
A lighthouse beam slices the dusk,
intent on an uninterrupted path.

The flashlight of the sky, forever
hunting for its elusive companion.

4th of July

The rain begins to pound
every available surface,
commanding as a war drum.

Perhaps rain is not always
a show of anger,
as Mother says.
Perhaps it is sorrowful,
or perhaps it is a blessing.

There will be no fireworks
tonight, no dogs
fleeing secure houses in terror,
no veterans with closed eyes,
hunched shoulders and clenched fists,
the television on too loud
and not loud enough.

Desert Lake

I walk down past the edge of the grass—
The drop off into the sudden desert to rest
Cautiously on the crumbling bricks that used
To make up one of the four walls of this home.

I close my eyes, try to imagine the life of its
Former residents. Every time, floating forms
Attack my lids, bang against the corners, springing
From one end to the other like acrobats, ridiculous

With their trailing bubbles, trapped air clinging to
Trapped flesh, wild animals caught in the serrated
Edges of my eyelashes. Why can't they be calm?
It would make the dying easier to watch.

Instead, they churn the air before me, force
Water out of my eyes and onto the dry sand
At my feet. Black starfish grow, stretch their
Limbs in the barren dust before retreating inward.

Tsunami

I was a child and she *was a child,*
  In this kingdom by the sea

—Edgar Allan Poe

I. Right-side up

The woman sits under the covered porch. Drops
ping off the top of the aluminum roof. As time passes,
the rain learns the language, alters its course to a slant,
manages a few seductive landings on her arm, her back.

The dewy grass taunts and entices, shimmering in the misty
morning.
She must admit, it does look fun. The squelch of mud between
toes,
the pleasant chill of diving feet-first into a black mirror.

II. Upside down

Slender clouds drift inches over the dense water
above the woman, now a child below the surface;
if heaven had cars, this is what it would look like—
parade of colorless cotton candy, just out of reach.

Dark fingers snake through the water to her,
suck the treat from her vision as her eyes blur.
The water is a cartoon Big Bad Wolf wound

backwards—no huffing and puffing, no blowing down. That is not good enough. It leaves things like her, the child, behind. This wolf is more efficient, inhaling it all, greedy whirlpool maw.

Feverish Delusions of a Walrus and a Carpenter

—inspired by Lewis Carroll

From scalp to sacrum and out,
the waves crash through me.

They chill the blood, immobilize the limbs. I close my
eyes and teeter in the chair, the vessel. At the front of the

room, the teacher talks of a play
while I focus on steering.

Another wave passes by, and I let out a slight moan, shift course
leeward. I rest my head momentarily on the hardwood desk,
unsure

if I can weather this internal
storm. The last thing I think
is why *the sea is boiling hot.*

It's a Metaphor, Darling

Imagine a whirlpool.
In it is a barrel.
There are more barrels
drifting around, sometimes
bumping into each other,
crossing paths.

Imagine two of the barrels
fuse together,
then three,
four.
They morph into a giant
rough triangle shape
which circles the eye,
drawing nearer
with each rotation.

Panic, grab a crowbar,
drive it into one of the barrels.
It breaks free.
Claw through the stomach—
mostly gunpowder
or ashes of cremation—
and a single bone.

The bone has a story
it wants to tell,
but it needs help,
someone to suck the marrow
out of the dark.

Below consciousness,
barrels are wrested
through the iris,
sand in an hourglass.

It is warmer here.
Turn to the side.
Eyes close and grains
crust the edges of lashes.
There is no waking, for you have
drowned in the sands of sleep.

Fin

The pond shivers at the speckled
brown leaf poised on its surface,
hidden in the shadows cast.

As time passes, the pond nudges the leaf,
studies the delicate veins that hold it together.

A tree never loses a single leaf.
Like a family, they fall in slow
syncopation on their own reflection.

When they meet again
years later in the murky abyss,
she asks if he is still old;
he asks if she is still young.

Downpour of Youth

She shifts her weight on the mattress,
thinks of the house that is her body. It's
old and rusty, no longer as sleek and polished
as it once was. Her skin is cracked and flaking
like the bark of a sycamore; some spots are white,
others are dark, colored with blossoming bruises
born from the air. They spread over her veins,
creep up the walls of her house.

An idea comes to her, and she plants
her feet on the floor, shuffles to the
door. *Silly girl*, she says to herself,
*plants grow old and die when they go
too long without water.* She unbolts the
wood and moves out into the storm. The
rain drums against her and she laughs, tilts
her head toward the sky to catch the rejuvenating
drops in the crevices of her face, the basin for the elixir.